TEACH ME, LORD

ALVIN G. LEWIS

Alvin G. Lewis

AUGSBURG PUBLISHING HOUSE
MINNEAPOLIS, MINNESOTA

TEACH ME, LORD

Copyright © 1976 Augsburg Publishing House

Library of Congress Catalog Card No. 76-3879

International Standard Book No. 0-8066-1535-4

All rights reserved. No part of this book may be used or reproduced in any manner whatsoever without written permission except in the case of brief quotations embodied in critical articles and reviews. For information address Augsburg Publishing House, 426 South Fifth Street, Minneapolis, Minnesota 55415.

Scripture quotations unless otherwise noted are from the Revised Standard Version of the Bible, copyright 1946, 1952, and 1971 by the Division of Christian Education of the National Council of Churches.

MANUFACTURED IN THE UNITED STATES OF AMERICA

Contents

Preface	9
The Power of God's Word	10
Apprehended by God	12
Lest He Go Away	14
Love Puts God First	16
Secure in God's Hands	18
A Reverent Tongue	20
Let God Be God	22
An Open-Door Policy	24
Time for Quiet Looking Up	26
Time Out for Rest	28
Learning to Cope	30
Citizenship Training	32
Life Is Precious	34
The Power of Example	36
Healing Therapy of Love	38
Laundered Thoughts	40
God's Cradle on Earth	42
God's Ownership	44

Our Guardianship	46
Words Can Be Arrows	48
Look at Their Good Side	50
Great Gain	52
A Just and Holy God	54
A Silver Lining	56
Who Is God?	58
The Only God	60
Three in His Oneness	62
Our Loving Heavenly Father	64
A Gift and a Promise	66
A Crisis and a Miracle	68
Poise or Panic	70
Praise in Action	72
Led by a Child	74
God's Work for Me	76
A Man Who Is God	78
The God Who Was Man	80
A Double Ownership	82

Pattern of Perfection	84
Such Love Is Costly	86
His Grave and Mine	88
To the Enemy's Capitol	90
God Said Amen	92
Homeward Bound	94
Our Spokesman in Heaven	96
What Time Is It?	98
Our Master Teacher	100
Where We Cannot Go	102
Under His Rule	104
A Total Commitment	106
God's Work in Me	108
About Face	110
Believing Is Seeing	112
Undeserved Merit	114
A New Beginning	116
Christian Maturity	118
Like a Mighty Army	120

The Foundation of Our Faith	122
A Glorious Body	124
Before God's Throne	126
Prayer Practices	128
Prayer Privileges	130
A Holy God	132
A Chain Reaction	134
A Difficult Prayer	136
Cause for Gratitude	138
A Dangerous Prayer	140
Times of Testing	142
Final Security	144
Prayer Power	146
A One-Sentence Gospel	148
Streams of God's Grace	150
A Memorial	152
A Testimony	154
Proof of Forgiveness	156
Hungry and Thirsty	158

To the glory of God
and with thanks to a dear wife and son
without whose love and inspiration
these pages would never have been written.

Preface

Through many years of parish ministry and a period of specialized ministry to those of advanced years and of failing eyesight, I have come to realize that for most people learning need never cease. Precious truths learned in childhood increase in value as the years go by, and a longing to rehearse them is a natural response. To facilitate such continued study this book has been written—to present a summary of basic scriptural teachings in clear, readily legible print.

The Revised Standard Version of the Bible was used throughout, except as otherwise indicated. The prayers at the end of each devotion are brief and personal. Inasmuch as these devotions will be used primarily by our senior Christians, I have used the traditional "thee" and "thou" in the prayers.

I pray that these devotions may bring the joy of renewal in the Christian instruction you received in childhood, and that Jesus Christ may continue to be your Savior and Lord through all your days.

The Power of God's Word

I am not ashamed of the gospel: for it is the power of God for salvation. ROMANS 1:16

We live in a world controlled by power—political, financial, atomic, oil. The power struggle is everywhere. But there is a power greater than this. It is the power of God's Word, a book written by humans, but inspired by God. Here is power which, when let loose in the hearts of men, wields a mighty transforming influence. It brings us face to face with our sin. It leads us to the cross of our Savior, Jesus Christ. It tells of God's love, which destroys despair and revives hope. It kindles love in our hearts for our brothers in need. Its transforming power is always at work.

Bishop Johannes Astrup, sainted missionary in South Africa, told the story about the power of

God's Word in his ministry. One of his mission stations maintained a home for orphaned and unwanted children. He told of one young girl whom they brought to the home in a most pitiable state. The practice was to photograph those brought to the home, and then to repeat the process at certain intervals. Interested in the progress of this particular girl, Dr. Astrup asked to see her photographs. Holding her first picture in one hand, and the most recent one, taken a few years later, in the other, he marvelled, "You wouldn't believe they were the same person." And, "What made the difference?" he asked.

"It was the power of God's Word at work in her life."

Almighty God, release, I pray, the power of the gospel in my life each day. Amen.

Apprehended by God

The righteousness of God has been manifested apart from law . . . the righteousness of God through faith in Jesus Christ. ROMANS 3:21-22

We are apprehended, that is arrested, not by the long arm of the law, but by the loving arm of God. God wants to control our lives, so he has shown us by his law how we are to behave as his children. Yet the best his law can do for us is to convince us how utterly impossible it is for us to do God's will perfectly.

This is the greatest blessing of God's law. Right at the moment of our deepest distress at falling short, God's law drives us to the One who has kept it perfectly on our behalf, our blessed Savior, Jesus Christ.

A pastor was explaining this lesson to his class. Mount Sinai represents the law, he taught them. It is high and rugged. It is too difficult for any of us to climb. But then if we look more closely we will discover two lone footprints which go up, up and completely over the top of this rugged mountain. Our Savior has made conquest of God's law. He has kept his Father's will perfectly. He went where we cannot go. His righteousness becomes ours by faith.

Therefore, when we feel sad because we have failed to do God's will, let us remember that God in Christ extends his loving arm about us. He wants us to know what his perfect will is so we may discover where we have strayed, that in Christ there is forgiveness for the past, and guidance for the steps ahead.

Dear Savior, always keep me in thy perfect righteousness. I need thine arm of love to support me. Help me to walk day by day in thy strength. Amen.

Lest He Go Away

How can I do this great wickedness and sin against God?   GENESIS 39:9

Real obedience comes from the inside. It is not something we can put on or off. This is what Martin Luther taught when he wrote that "we should fear and love God," and so keep God's commandments. In the first commandment he added a third word—trust.

We should fear God, it says. Mrs. Jones was honestly puzzled about this. One day she confided to her nurse, "I don't think we should fear God."

The nurse had a good reply. "My pastor taught me," she said, "that when we fear only God's punishment we fear lest God comes. This is to be afraid of God. But when we have child-like fear of God we fear lest God will go away."

This is the way Joseph in the Old Testament felt when tempted to do evil. He said, "How can I do this great wickedness and sin against God?" His obedience came from his heart. He truly feared his God.

A young farm lad, at home alone one day, was throwing stones at the flock of geese in the barnyard. To his horror one stone hit and killed the largest gander. Quickly the boy buried the bird, then anxiously awaited his parents' return—not happily, but with fear, fear lest they come to punish.

With his forgiveness our blessed Savior has removed such fear. He has entered the picture of our greatest need, and says to us, "Come to me."

Heavenly Father, help me to put thee first in my life always. Amen.

Love Puts God First

If you love me, you will keep my commandments. JOHN 14:15

How can I love God above all things? At best our ability and capacity to love God is limited. But we have a beautiful example in the love of Jesus. St. John wrote, "We love because he first loved us."

Because Jesus loved his father he did his Father's will. If we love God we will keep his commandments. This is the kind of love that requires obedience. Love and obedience cannot be separated. Pastor Karl Rest told of a bold preacher who once said to his congregation, "Too many people love God the way they love their cow. They love their cow for the milk, butter, cheese and profit she gives them." In the same way many of us love God only for what we get from him. Actually this can be nothing more than self-love. This is like the willful child who seeks his parents' favor only for the good things they give him. But there the relationship ceases. He wouldn't think of lifting a finger to help or comfort them. Our Father in heaven wants us to love him, and prove it by what we can do for him.

We need to guard against those things that come between God and us. It is so easy to allow what we own, what we do, what we worry about —anything—to occupy our hearts and take God's place. Our love for God will control these situations, and keep God in first place where he belongs.

Send thy Holy Spirit, dear Father, to create love continually in my heart. Help me to show my love in daily obedience to thy will, and in showing charity towards others. Amen.

Secure in God's Hands

Though he slay me, yet will I trust in him.

JOB 13:15 KJV

Job was about at the end of his rope. He had suffered so much. He had lost his health, his property, his neighbors' good will, and even his children. Now his most intimate friends and his wife were giving him a hard time. This would be enough to shatter anyone's faith, and yet, tempted as he was to turn his back on his Maker, Job valiantly proclaimed, "Though he slay me, yet will I trust in him." We have heard them tell of the patience of Job. Perhaps we should think also of his unshakeable trust in God.

There are many Jobs in the world, challenged by distress or disaster on the one hand, or by over-abundance on the other. Trust is put to the test. Perhaps we feel betrayed by God, or that we scarcely need him. There are many in both categories of life today.

These and other difficult circumstances need not destroy our trust in God. Like Job we can continue to rely on God's never-failing promises and place all our concerns in his hands. He is our faithful Father, who is aware of all our needs, whether our situation in life is easy or difficult.

When life's problems confront us, Hebrews 12 reminds us, "The Lord disciplines him whom he loves." We can trust him and know that he is dealing with us in love and wisdom. Then all is well.

Kind Heavenly Father, I thank thee for all thy blessings. Whether life is easy or difficult, help me to trust. Amen.

A Reverent Tongue

He who is mighty has done great things for me, and holy is his name.   LUKE 1:49

The names of God underscore everything we know about Him. He is Jehovah, Jesus, Christ, Spirit, Lord. He is Father, Almighty, Conqueror, Savior, Prophet, Priest, King, Word, Brother, Master, Teacher, Shepherd, Friend, Alpha, Omega, Gracious, Merciful, Good. He creates, preserves, provides, protects, forgives, rescues, sanctifies, saves. What a wonderful God we have! His names are holy and precious.

How sad and shocking it is to hear these names used in levity and profanity. Almost daily on TV and radio these holy names are abused. For many this is becoming a part of their casual conversation.

Bishop Lunde of Norway told the story of a man who had bursts of anger and profanity.

One day out in the back yard, unaware that his young son was within earshot, he lost his temper. He began to beat his horse to the accompaniment of profane words. That evening as mother and father sat quietly by the fireside, they heard the little boy upstairs. He was beating his wooden horse and shouting the profanities he had heard his father use. Needless to say, that father was convicted of his own misuse of God's name and the chain reaction which resulted.

God wants us to use his name with all the many blessings it implies. He invites us to tell him our needs and to thank and praise him. Mary, the mother of Jesus, showed us a good example when she reverently responded, "He who is mighty has done great things for me, and holy is his name."

Dear Father, help me always to use thy name with honor and reverence. Amen.

Let God Be God

In all thy ways acknowledge him, and he shall direct thy paths. PROVERBS 3:6 KJV

"I wonder what lies ahead? What's around the corner?" How often we have said or thought that, and wished we could do something about it. How easy it is, when we entertain such thoughts, to want to take things into our own hands.

This was the experience of King Saul of the Old Testament. When his days were uncertain and he was experiencing one reverse after another, he was determined to find out what the future might bring. Instead of acknowledging God and asking his direction, Saul went to the nearest fortune-teller — the witch of Endor. From that day on Saul's fortunes deteriorated.

There are many today like King Saul who cannot wait for God to direct their paths. Instead they go to fortune-tellers, astrologers, necromancers, seances, or readers of tea leaves, coffee grounds, or palms. Reports have indicated that whenever our country experiences a crisis, these black-magic vendors multiply and they have a surge of business.

God has wisely dropped a curtain between us and the future. He asks us to trust him, to have faith in his direction. Abraham, another of our Old Testament heroes, displayed this faith. When God asked him to leave his homeland to enter a strange land, he humbly followed God's direction even though he did not know where God was taking him. He let God be God in his life and was confident of the future which God would supply. His life was enriched and blessed.

Bless me, Father, with faith enough to look only to thee for my future. Amen.

An Open-Door Policy

Behold, thou desirest truth in the inward being.   PSALM 51:6

Loyalty to truth is a virtue that binds character together. When St. Paul was describing the Christian's armor in Ephesians 6 he began by telling us that we should "buckle up the belt of truth" (Phillips). Obviously it was this belt which held the whole armor in place. Truth is fundamental to one's personal peace, as well as one's happy associations with others.

As Christians we represent the name of God. To break or stretch the truth, therefore, reflects on his name. Ananias and Sapphira in the book of Acts tried to raise a false front for themselves by distorting the truth, and the result was disaster. A lie caused their downfall.

Jane was a new employee at a textile factory. Her instructions were to notify her supervisor immediately if her machine became entangled. At first all went well. She wanted to impress her superiors so she tried to appear efficient. Then one day the inevitable happened. The thread in her machine became slightly tangled. She thought she could fix it. Embarrassed, she tried to cover up her trouble. But the more she tried to justify her slow-up the worse things became. Finally her machine broke down completely, and she had to face a justly indignant supervisor. Jane's attempt to cover up her problem got her into difficulty.

We all are quite able cover-up actors when it comes to manipulating truth to our own convenience. At the cross we can find forgiveness, and grace to be sincerely truthful.

Dear Lord, guard my heart and my lips that my words and my life may honor thy name. Amen.

Time for Quiet Looking Up

Blessed are those who hear the Word of God and keep it.   LUKE 11:28

Going to God's house for worship and hearing the message of his Word is like a ship entering the locks of a canal. Burdened with its cargo the ship enters the lock. The gates are closed behind it, and the waters from above pour in. Lifted upward by this flow from above, the ship soon continues its journey on a higher level.

Voltaire, the atheistic philosopher, once said, "You can only destroy the Christian religion when you first destroy the Sunday observance." This enemy of our faith apparently realized better than do some who hold it dear, how vital is our regular worship.

In the Old Testament God's people were commanded to worship on the seventh day. God's command to us is, "Worship!" All days in the New Testament are holy. Therefore the early Christians chose the first day of the week for worship to remember and honor Christ's resurrection, and the coming of the Holy Spirit. Unable to detach themselves from the Old Testament commandment to worship, some people have tried to make Sunday an Old Testament sabbath by keeping certain rules.

God asks us to worship him, and to hear his Word. We need moral and spiritual recharging. We need to hear often the message of God's redemptive love in Christ, our Savior. Thus, permitting this inspiration from above to flow into our hearts, we are lifted, reassured, and strengthened to continue confidently on our way.

Support me, Father, in my resolve to worship thee, to hear thy Word and obey it. Amen.

Time Out for Rest

The sabbath was made for man, not man for the sabbath.   MARK 2:27

Through his death and resurrection our Savior has completely fulfilled all the Old Testament ceremonial laws, including the one which dealt with the sabbath. St. Paul explained this in Colossians 2, "Let no one pass judgment on you in questions of food and drink or with regard to a festival or . . . a sabbath. These are only a shadow of what is to come; but the substance belongs to Christ." The New Testament church chose the first day of the week as the day of worship. It was the day made special by the resurrection of Jesus and by the coming of the Holy Spirit.

In the creation God knew there would be a limit to human physical endurance. He warned that people would need to take time for rest. God instructed them to work six days, then to follow his creation example and rest one day. We need regular time for rest and relaxation to restore body and mind. In our time it seems this day of rest has become either another day of work or an excuse for celebration.

A survey taken a few years ago by one of our American corporations showed the employees' lowest rate of efficiency was on Monday. Obviously these people came to work exhausted after their day of "rest." God ordered a day of rest, not that we can make the day holy by what we do or do not do, but that we may permit the day to restore us as we rest and worship him.

Sustain me both in body and mind, dear God, and help me use the day of rest for that purpose. Amen.

Learning to Cope

Children, obey your parents in the Lord, for this is right. EPHESIANS 6:1

One of the most difficult lessons in life to learn is respect for authority. Parents teach this early in life through firm, loving discipline.

God has delegated his authority to parents and others who are responsible for conduct. As we respond to authority imposed in love, we receive two blessings. First, we learn that God directs our lives, and second, we learn to live in harmony with the world around us. Without discipline, life is just one continuous experience of resentment and rebellion.

Our homes need the Bible. There we see Jesus' perfect obedience to his parents. There we find inspiration to love one another. In it we learn God's will for our lives.

A worried father came to his pastor. "My boy wants to run away from home. What shall I do?"

"Tell him I want to see him," the pastor replied. The boy came. After discussing his problem, the pastor told the boy, "Run away if you wish, but I want to read something to you first." From the Bible the pastor read the story of the prodigal son. Turning to the boy, he said, "Good-bye, son, I hope you have a good trip."

Several days later the pastor met the boy on the street. "I thought you ran away."

"No," replied the lad, "the story you read to me just wouldn't let me go." A story of love from God's Word made the difference.

Dear God, send thy love into the homes of our land. Amen.

Citizenship Training

Let every person be subject to the governing authorities. For there is no authority except from God. ROMANS 13:1

Behind the picture of juvenile delinquency and the rising crime rate in our country is a state of general permissiveness. It is the story of retreating parenthood and of willful children who seldom if ever have felt the gentle but firm hand of God-given authority.

The pastor was called to the home of a fourteen-year-old lad in his congregation. The parents were in near frustration over the boy's disobedience. He refused to be controlled, kept bad company, and roamed the streets at night. Unfortunately, the parents could not agree on how to impose authority. The pastor counseled with the family, but the problem persisted. Later one evening the mother in tears appeared at the pastor's door. The police had just taken their son to jail for stealing and house-prowling.

If we learn respect for authority imposed with love in our homes during childhood, we can better live within the law later in life. Training for good citizenship is training in accepting the discipline of love at home. From this home-training comes the realization that the authority of God stands behind the authority of the state.

Our Savior was obedient to his father's will. He also submitted to the authority of his parents and the state. By his conduct and his teachings Jesus left us a picture of obedience to the law of the land. He was a good citizen.

Watch over our country, O God, that our citizens may early learn the lessons of obedience to law. Amen.

Life Is Precious

He who loves his neighbor has fulfilled the law.
ROMANS 13:8

It is easy and convenient to feel that we have never violated the commandment, "Thou shalt not kill."

A young man was in the hospital following an accident in which one of his legs was badly broken. He was a bitter young man, angry at the one he thought caused the accident, unhappy with his hospital care and with life in general. When his father tried to comfort him by describing the good recovery of others undergoing similar treatment, the lad flew into a rage.

His roommate was a Christian. Later, when the two roommates were discussing their daily lives, their conversation turned to the Ten Commandments. "There's only one commandment I haven't broken," the young man said, boastfully, "Thou shalt not kill."

His roommate responded, "Remember, the Bible says, 'Anyone who hates his brother is a murderer.'" He did not need to say any more.

Life is our most precious earthly possession. We know that the destruction of life is a sin, and we are repulsed by the very thought of it. But we must also guard against anger which leads to this sin. Cain killed his brother Abel, but the Bible first says Cain was angry. Hatred leads to destruction of life, but love is the protector of life.

Our Savior is the ideal here. When his enemies hated him, he loved them in return. He won his victory, and ours, through love.

Lord and Giver of life, help me to protect and use this precious gift to thy glory. Amen.

The Power of Example

Let your light so shine before men, that they may see your good works and give glory to your Father who is in heaven. MATTHEW 5:16

A missionary to China some years ago found it impossible to learn the Chinese language. As a result, he requested permission to return home. The native Chinese who had learned to know this missionary objected.

The reason for their objection came to the surface one day when a meeting of catechumens was in progress. The leader of the meeting asked if anyone could tell what it means to be a Christian. A hand was raised at the rear of the room. The answer was, "It means to be like our missionary."

This missionary had never been able to preach a single sermon in the Chinese language. He had not even spoken to anyone in that language. Yet the power of his Christian example had been so strong that the people wanted to be like him.

In a sense we all are missionaries every day. With our example we can cause others to be led into the Christian life, and to give glory to God. We are reminded of the descriptive verse which speaks convincingly of this:

> Matthew, Mark, Luke and John,
> Gospels good and true;
> But the only gospel some folks read
> Is the gospel according to you.

God calls us to walk day by day with our Savior, and to ask his help to be lights in this dark world.

Gracious Lord, forgive the bad examples I have set, and help me to let thy light burn brightly in me. Amen.

Healing Therapy of Love

Love covers a multitude of sins.   I PETER 4:8

There is no commandment which covers such a broad scope as "Thou shalt not kill." From negative to positive its admonition progresses all the way from forbidding murder, to going out of our way to help others. It shows the danger of hatred, and finally admonishes us to be active in love on our neighbor's behalf. As with each of the others this commandment convicts us all. It really is a powerful lesson on how to conquer with love.

St. Paul has described love best, "Love is patient and kind; love is not jealous or boastful; it is not arrogant or rude. Love does not insist on its own way." Love is always ready to sacrifice.

John was a humble child of God, and wanted to love everyone. One day he noticed that someone was stealing his hay. He suspected who it was, and when he followed the wheel tracks, he found it was the wayward son of a good friend. The next night John was waiting nearby when the culprit pulled up beside his hay stack. After the intruder began to load hay on his rack, John took his pitchfork, climbed onto the hay stack and, without a word, started pitching hay too. Although the young man protested, John did not stop until the rack was well loaded. We might think John had every right to show anger at the young man. Yet he followed the pattern of his Savior, and conquered by love. Sin yielded to love.

Kind Heavenly Father, forgive my hatred. Help me to conquer with love. Amen.

Laundered Thoughts

Blessed are the pure in heart for they shall see God.
MATTHEW 5:8

Some years ago New York City faced a possible epidemic of typhoid fever. Experts found the cause of the problem in Croton Lake which, at the time, supplied the city's water. The city health department immediately began a water purification program, using filtration and chemicals. They were not successful until they cleaned up the filthy conditions in the watershed above the lake, at its source.

To keep the commandment, "Thou shalt not commit adultery," Luther admonishes us to "lead a chaste and pure life in word and deed." Perhaps we feel we have not disobeyed this commandment. However, our Savior said, "Everyone who looks at a woman lustfully has already committed adultery with her in his heart." When they brought the adulteress to Jesus, his response was, "Let him who is without sin be the first to throw a stone at her." We all stand convicted.

How can we obey this commandment and remove the source of temptation? Proverbs says, "As a man thinketh . . . so is he." The call is for pure thoughts. We can eliminate the source of evil by constant use of God's Word and prayer, by wholesome companions, and by worthwhile use of our time.

For those who bear the guilt of sin against this commandment, and desire God's forgiveness, let us remember the words of St. Paul concerning adulterers, "But you were washed . . . you were justified in the name of the Lord Jesus Christ."

Guard my mind, dear God, and help me think only pure thoughts. Amen.

God's Cradle on Earth

Greet the church in their house.   ROMANS 16:5

Apparently Prisca and Aquila, fellow-workers of the Apostle Paul, were among the most faithful in Rome. In fact, it seems that the church centered in their home. It was a rallying place for Christians in an otherwise pagan community. In this home Christians gathered to worship and pray and to encourage each other in the faith. Within its walls many no doubt found refuge from the evils of persecution.

During the pioneer days in our country, much the same practice was followed. Christians offered their homes as places of worship. Before churches were built, homes were the centers for Christian fellowship, Bible study, and prayer. Like Prisca and Aquila they had "church in their house." In our day, too, groups of Christians gather in homes to witness, study, and pray.

We need a church in every home. There Jesus is the Head of the house. There parents teach their children to pray and to know God's Word. A Christian home is God's cradle on earth where his children are nurtured in the Christian faith.

God has set the home and the family as the foundation of Christian culture. Without them, Christian civilization, as we know it, will disappear. One of the greatest threats of the home today is divorce. God gave the commandment "Thou shalt not commit adultery" to guard and preserve the Christian family and home. When Christ is the Head of our homes, and God's Word is loved, homes are blessed.

Dear Jesus, be the Head of my house. Come in and dwell here. Amen.

God's Ownership

What have you that you did not receive?

I CORINTHIANS 4:7

Job in the Old Testament was one of the world's richest men. He believed, however, that all he had came from God. After it was all taken from him, he exclaimed, "Naked I came from my mother's womb and naked shall I return; the Lord gave and the Lord has taken away: blessed be the name of the Lord."

Although it is true that we work for what we have, still it comes to us from God. Our money and property, health and strength, time and talents, all come to us from God. He graciously distributes these gifts among us, to some more, to others less.

It is right that we should work for what we receive. It is not our right to take what God has given to someone else. Much of the trouble in the world today comes from our meddling with God's distribution of property. We want to take matters into our own hands and grasp what is given to someone else. This happens not only with individuals but also with business interests and nations.

Stealing can assume many forms. We break the commandment "Thou shalt not steal" if we take what belongs to another, or if we waste what is our own. If we are unfaithful or lazy at work, neglect honest debts, underpay our help, overcharge, or cheat, we are guilty of stealing. If, however, we are content with what God gives us as a result of honest labor, and use it carefully, we will experience God's rich blessing upon what we have.

Help me, dear Father, to be happy with thy gifts, and use them to thy glory. Amen.

Our Guardianship

It is required of stewards that they be found trustworthy.   I CORINTHIANS 4:2

God has a reason for everything. According to Ephesians 4, God's purpose in giving us the opportunity to work is that we may be able to help others when there is need. The Apostle Paul is telling us that we should do "honest work with our hands so that we may be able to give to those in need."

God has made us guardians or caretakers. We are to supervise certain talents and properties on his behalf. This means that we are in debt to others because we are endowed by God. It becomes our duty to help our neighbor keep and protect his property. It also is our duty to use what God has given us to help where there is need.

It was July Fourth and the Smith family was leaving for the day. As they drove away, they noticed that the neighbor's cattle were escaping from the pasture through a broken fence. They knew their neighbor was not at home. Although it was inconvenient for him and his family, Mr. Smith rounded up the cattle and repaired the fence. He helped protect his neighbor's property.

The church is God's work. To accomplish its great program of mission and charity it needs support. God's command is to bring the Christian gospel to the whole world and to show the love of Christ to those in need. To give to this work in God's kingdom is an act of worship. When we realize how great Christ's love is for us, supporting his work becomes a thrilling experience.

Lord, help me to be a good steward of thy gifts. Make me trustworthy. Amen.

Words Can Be Arrows

Let all bitterness and wrath and anger and clamor and slander be put away from you, with all malice.   EPHESIANS 4:31

Basil Rathbone once told this story. A young British officer in World War I stopped to chat with a group of British artillerymen on the Western front. He asked permission to fire their cannon. Immediately the Germans retaliated with a single shot which fell into a British dugout, killing four men. One of the four was the brother of this young British officer who had so casually fired the first shot. That young officer was Rathbone himself. He never ceased to regret that random shot.

So it is with words. Careless, thoughtless words often bounce back, bringing heartache and pain. Like poisoned arrows they leave resentment and bitterness in someone's heart. Although they may have been spoken thoughtlessly or in a flare of temper rather than with deliberate malice, they can never be recalled.

One's reputation is a precious possession. Realizing this, we need to pray for grace to protect this gift with words that are careful and kind.

Jane had told a false story about Ruth. Soon everyone knew. One day when they were together, Jane apologized and asked forgiveness. "Of course I forgive you," Ruth said. Then stooping, she picked a dandelion which had a large, fluffy head of seeds. Ruth blew the seeds into the wind, then said, "Now Jane, can you pick up those seeds for me?"

Jane understood. "Thoughts unexpressed may sometimes drop back dead, but only God can kill them when they're said."

Kind Heavenly Father, send thy Holy Spirit to guard my tongue. Amen.

Look at Their Good Side

Be kind to one another, tenderhearted, forgiving one another, as God in Christ forgave you.

EPHESIANS 4:32

A preacher once said that the difference between breaking and keeping the commandment "Thou shalt not bear false witness against thy neighbor" is the difference between a buzzard and a bee. The buzzard flies high over head looking for something dead or decaying. It delights to feast on something rotten, and then to carry the decay and germs far and wide. The honeybee, on the other hand, wings its way from flower to flower, seeking only sweetness, with which it creates more sweetness for others to enjoy. On its way it carries pollen which breeds and multiplies fragrance and beauty of fruit and flower.

Many people are like that. Some are searching the lives of others to find something bad to feed on, then carry evil around to others. Martin Luther once said, "The slanderer has the devil in his tongue, and the listener has him in his ear." Thank God there are many, on the contrary, who try to see only the virtues in others. The story they carry is sweetness and kindness, fruitfulness and beauty. Are we buzzards or bees?

How much better to look at the good side. St. Paul points to the beautiful life of Jesus, to his kindness and forgiveness. The climax of his challenge to would-be gossipers comes when he says, "As God in Christ forgave you." When Jesus died to forgive us completely, what right have we to magnify the sins of others? It is much better to approach others with hearts of forgiveness, observing from a constructive point of view.

Lord, give me a forgiving heart, a kind tongue, and a discerning ear. Amen.

Great Gain

There is great gain in godliness with contentment.   I TIMOTHY 6:6

Of course, we may desire good things, and there is nothing wrong with this. But sinful coveting is jealousy of others' good fortune and the desire to possess what is theirs. No one can be contented and happy in such a state.

King Ahab and Queen Jezebel in the Old Testament are examples of sinful coveting, and what it leads to. Ahab was so covetous of his neighbor's vineyard that it became an obsession. As a result, Ahab and his scheming queen broke at least seven of the commandments, and experienced nothing but unhappiness, and tragedy.

The commandment "Thou shalt not covet" teaches us the importance of contentment. If we love God and do his will, we will love our neighbor and be happy with our place in life. This is contentment. This is what God intended for us.

Fanny Crosby, the great hymn-writer, is a good example. She was blind from the sixth week of her life. Yet because she loved her Savior, she was always a happy person. At age eight she wrote:

O what a happy soul I am!
Although I cannot see,
I am resolved that in this world
Contented I will be.

How many blessings I enjoy,
That other people don't;
To weep and sigh because I'm blind,
I cannot and I won't.

To Fanny Crosby, having Christ was complete contentment. The result was great gain for herself and for the world. Her 8000 hymns have brought blessing to many.

Be always near me, dear Savior, and fill my life with happiness and contentment. Amen.

A Just and Holy God

You shall be holy; for I the Lord your God am holy.

LEVITICUS 19:2

Philip Nolan is remembered as "The Man Without a Country." In the early 1800s under the influence of Aaron Burr, this young army officer developed a rebellious attitude against America. Before a court of reprimand he made a reckless wish that he would never hear of the United States again. For his wrong he was sentenced to spend the rest of his life at sea. No one was ever to speak of America in his presence. For 46 years, until he died and was buried at sea, Nolan was transferred from one American ship to another. He never saw his homeland again.

During those years Philip Nolan learned many lessons. At first bitter, he mellowed and came to long for and love his country. He learned to respect her laws. He studied and sought information of home. He gathered pictures and literature of America. He became a humble, penitent, Bible-reading Christian.

We learn from the Bible that God is a just and holy God. Our sinful ways and God's justice and holiness are brought into sharp contrast. We discover that without him we are homeless, and spiritually at sea. Our just and holy God must require obedience to his will and pronounce judgment on our sin. He gives his blessing when we obey.

Philip Nolan was never forgiven by his country. But God has provided for our complete forgiveness and final return to our heavenly homeland, because Jesus came to give his life for us.

God, forgive my sins for Jesus' sake and help me to do thy will. Amen.

A Silver Lining

Christ redeemed us from the curse of the law.
GALATIANS 3:13

The story of sin began in the garden of Eden. Our first parents, sinless from creation, disobeyed the one restriction God had placed on them. Every human has inherited a sinful nature as a result of this first sin. David wrote in Psalm 51, "Behold I was brought forth in iniquity, and in sin did my mother conceive me." From this inherited sinful state come all our problems of sin, including sickness, sorrow, suffering and death. St. Paul explains our dilemma, "I know that nothing good dwells within me. . . . I do not do the good I want, but the evil I do not want is what I do."

Is there no way out of this terrible problem of sin? Yes, thank God there is! To this Paul writes, "Wretched man that I am! Who shall deliver me? . . . Thanks be to God through Jesus Christ our Lord! . . . There is now no condemnation for those who are in Christ Jesus."

One day Johnny was a naughty boy. As his father was leaving he told Johnny that he must hoe the entire garden that day or he would be punished. The boy tried, but he could see the task was too great for him. Just when he felt defeated, his big brother came to the rescue and completed the job. When the father returned, there was no punishment. Johnny's big brother had accomplished the work the younger boy could not do. Just so, Jesus our Brother has taken our place.

Thanks, Lord Jesus, for doing what I could not do, for thy mercy and love. Amen.

Who Is God?

I trust in thee, O Lord, I say, "Thou are my God."
                                            PSALM 31:14

What kind of a God is this and how can we know him? There are three sources of information. We can look around us at his beautiful creation and discover as the psalmist said, "The heavens are telling the glory of God, and the firmament proclaims his handiwork." We can be sensitive to the voice of God in our conscience, which prompts us to do his will. But most of all we find God revealed in Holy Scripture.

The Bible teaches us that God revealed himself as a person. We never call God it, but he. He is a creator God, who has formed the world, including man, the holy angels, and all of life. This creation God preserves, protects, and provides for. He is eternal and almighty. He is everywhere present and all-knowing. He is holy, wise, and good.

Our God is a Savior-God. As our loving Father he sent his Son, Jesus Christ, to redeem fallen man from sin and hell. God is merciful and gracious. Psalm 103 says, "As the heavens are high above the earth, so great is his love toward those who fear him." Astronomers tell us that if we were to reach the nearest galaxy of stars in the heavens we would have to shoot straight up into space at the speed of light, 186,000 miles per second, and travel for 800,000 years. This gives us some idea of the limitless love of God. It is simply beyond our comprehension. Such a God we have. We can only approach him in faith.

Blessed God, help me to say and believe that thou art my God. Amen.

The Only God

For there is one God. 2 TIMOTHY 2:5

Haifa in Israel is a beautiful city on the shores of the blue Mediterranean. Part of the city is built on the slopes of Mount Carmel. It was on that mountain many years ago in the Old Testament that Elijah, the prophet, engaged the 450 prophets of Baal, the heathen god, in a contest which was to prove that the God of Israel is the only God. The prophets of Baal tried desperately but failed to get response to their sacrifice. In answer to their prayers there was only silence. Elijah, however, received a powerful response to his offering and prayers. God established himself as the only true God (1 Kings 18:20-40).

When the Apostle Paul was at the Areopagus in Athens, Greece, he noticed that the place was full of altars to many gods. Standing in the midst of this scene Paul spoke. His fearless message was on behalf of the God, who was designated as "an unknown god." Paul wasted no time in making our God known, and in pointing to him as the only true God, the Father of Jesus Christ, whom he raised from the dead (Acts 17:16-30).

There are still many gods in the world. Some of them are worshiped at altars. Others, more subtle and having no altars, nevertheless hold strong control over people. Some of their names are money, property, careers, amusements. The voices of Elijah and Paul need to be heard in our day. When we say, "I believe in God the Father," and mean it, we are enthroning the only true God in our hearts.

Come into my heart, Lord, and rule there as the only God. Amen.

Three in His Oneness

The grace of the Lord Jesus Christ and the love of God and the fellowship of the Holy Spirit be with you all. 2 CORINTHIANS 13:14

While Scripture teaches that there is only one God, it pictures God as a Trinity. There are three persons in God, Father, Son and Holy Spirit, all perfectly equal, all true God. How this can be is a mystery, but a mystery substantiated by Scripture.

Although the Bible does not mention the word Trinity, it is everywhere taught. At the baptism of Jesus the three persons of the Godhead are vividly portrayed. We are commanded to baptize in the name of the Holy Trinity. The three persons are involved in the Apostolic Benediction. The Bible teaches that each person of the Trinity has special works on our behalf. The Father is the Creator, the Son is the Redeemer, and the Holy Spirit is the Sanctifier. Though distinct in their works, they are inseparable, each member of the Trinity participating in each evidence of God's power. Genesis 1 says that God created the world, the Spirit moved upon the waters; and John 1 says that without the Word, that is Jesus, nothing was created. Also in our salvation the Bible says that the Spirit works repentance and drives us to Christ who covers and forgives our guilt, and the Father gives us Christ's righteousness and declares us innocent.

A candle has one flame, yet there are three elements burning — wax, cotton, and air. The shamrock has one leaf, yet three distinct petals. So is the Holy Trinity, three in its oneness.

Holy Trinity of God, accomplish thy divine works in me. Amen.

Our Loving Heavenly Father

For God so loved the world that he gave his only Son, that whoever believes in him should not perish but have eternal life. JOHN 3:16

A father was distressed and hurt to see his son lose interest in the home situation and long to find happiness out in the far country. The boy left home and the father patiently waited and worried about his safety and well-being. No doubt he often looked down that empty road hoping there would be a sign of his son's return.

When we talk about the story of the prodigal son, the main emphasis is usually on the ambitious son who ran away, or his jealous brother who resented the prodigal's return. Actually, however, the most important person of this story is the patient, waiting father.

Knowing that his son was wandering far from home, the father longed to take him in his arms and shelter him from an evil world. Then came the day when, scanning the horizon, he saw a ragged, broken-down looking creature coming up the road. With eyes of love he quickly recognized his own son coming home. Running to meet him, the father welcomed him with open arms. All the bitterness was past now. The son was home again. The father's heart was glad.

This is the picture of our loving heavenly Father, our patient waiting Father. To fulfill his love and bring his wayward ones home he sent his Son to die on the cross. In his death Jesus took our place, and promises us life again in the Father's house.

Dear Father, I thank thee for sending Jesus to bring me home again. Amen.

A Gift and a Promise

In the beginning God created the heavens and the earth.   GENESIS 1:1

What was there in the beginning? Only God. Genesis says, "In the beginning God." In Psalm 90 Moses adds, "Before the mountains were brought forth or ever thou hadst formed the earth and the world, from everlasting to everlasting thou art God."

Out of a scene of nothingness the world began. God with his infinite power formed the heavens and the earth. The elements of light, air, soil, and plant life, the universe of planets and stars, life that inhabits air and water, animals that occupy the land, all came from God's creative hand.

The crown of God's creation was man, sinless, in God's image, with intelligence and an immortal soul. This and all of God's creation came by the power of his Word: "He spoke and it came to be, he commanded, and it stood forth."

The tragedy of this story is that man fell from the perfection of God's creation. The devil tempted, man yielded, and sin entered the world. Man became innately sinful and was separated from God. Immediately God provided a solution. He promised that Jesus Christ would come to earth to redeem fallen mankind.

When we say, "I believe that God has created me," we confess our faith that his creation continues even today. At the same time we are assured that though his creation has been blighted by sin, God's promise of grace, a Savior from sin, is ours too.

Heavenly Father, I thank thee for my body, and my soul, but most of all for Jesus, the Savior of my soul. Amen.

A Crisis and a Miracle

When they had eaten their fill, he told his disciples, "Gather up the fragments left over."
JOHN 6:12

There's a miracle in these words taken from the story of Jesus' feeding of the 5000. Since they were far from any source of supply, providing bread for so great a throng could have caused a crisis. Philip, one of the disciples, had given thought to this possibility when it was suggested that they divide up the lunch a young lad had brought. "Five loaves and two fish! For 5000 people?" Philip worried. "How many crumbs would that make for each one?" There was a crisis indeed.

Perhaps Philip would have made an accurate caterer, but he had neglected to take into account that God, the Provider, was present. Calmly Jesus, in essence, told them, "Just bring what you have to me." They did, and Jesus blessed it. When they distributed the bread they all ate "their fill," and had twelve baskets full left over!

What a picture of God's providence! We worry and fret about having enough, forgetting that all we have comes from God. If we could only learn the lesson to bring what we have to Jesus. God's hand has not been shortened. Then instead of spending our energies worrying or complaining, we could use them giving thanks and praise.

An old man, thinking these thoughts, once said, "There's too many singing, 'Nobody knows the trouble I've seen' and not enough singing, 'Glory, Hallelujah.' "

Heavenly Father, I thank thee for all thy many blessings. Amen.

Poise or Panic

The Lord is my shepherd. PSALM 23:1

The picture of the faithful shepherd watching over his flock best describes God's protecting care of his children. There are many lurking dangers. Yet the psalmist can declare, "I shall not want," "I shall not fear." What poise and security in the midst of uncertainty!

In this life we need constant security. Without it we become restless worriers. With the Good Shepherd we can face the problems of need and privation and say with David, "I shall not want."

Likewise, we need daily deliverance, or we become hopeless captives. The Good Shepherd delivers from the threat of temptations, reckless ambitions, uncertainties, and even of death and the grave. He interprets for us the words, "I shall not fear."

We also need a fixed goal, or we become aimless wanderers. The Good Shepherd holds before us the certainty of a home in heaven some day. We can say with the psalmist, "I shall dwell in the house of the Lord forever."

With that kind of watchful care, and with the confidence of forgiveness and salvation, life can become a happy experience each day.

The passengers of a sea-going vessel were experiencing fear at the turbulence of the water. The ship was tossing wildly. A small boy was playing quietly on the floor. One of the adults asked him, "Aren't you worried about the storm?"

The lad replied, "No, my dad is the pilot, so I know we are safe."

Quiet my fears, dear God, and help me fix my eyes on the goal of heaven. Amen.

Praise in Action

As you did it to one of the least of these my brethren, you did it to me.   MATTHEW 25:40

In his explanation of the first article Luther lists the unmerited blessings we receive from our heavenly Father and says, "For all which I am in duty bound to thank, praise, serve and obey him." With blessings come responsibilities. We praise and serve God in two ways, both in worship of him, and in helping those in need around us. One cannot exist without the other. We can never praise God sufficiently.

Our Savior identified himself with those in need. He called them "My brethren." When we help them we serve him.

This message is told in "The Vision of Sir Launfal," a dramatic story told by James Russell Lowell. One day a nobleman began his search for the Holy Grail. As he rode away from his castle, he carelessly tossed a gold coin at the beggar who sat at his gate. Many years passed. The nobleman finally returned. His life was spent, possessions gone, and he had not found the Holy Grail.

The beggar still sat at his gate. This time the nobleman stopped and divided his only crust of bread with the beggar. As the two ate, a light enveloped them. The nobleman realized that the Savior dwelt in the form of this beggar, who said, "Who gives himself with his alms feeds three, himself, his hungering neighbor and me." The nobleman had found the Holy Grail at his very gate.

From that time, with a heart now alert to the will of God, his greatest concern was for those in need.

God, I thank thee for all thy blessings. Create in me a love for others. Amen.

Led by a Child

To you is born this day in the city of David a Savior, who is Christ the Lord. LUKE 2:11

Caesar Augustus thought he was in charge when he made his decree. Actually he was only one link in a long chain of events that began unfolding long before he came on the scene. Prophecy after prophecy, through the centuries, had detailed the Bethlehem events.

A virgin had miraculously conceived by visitation of God's Spirit. Born in humble circumstances, but heralded by heavenly messengers, Jesus made his entry into the world. As the angelic host proclaimed, the coming of this little child has brought joy and transformation to people throughout the world.

There is a striking parallel between the Christmas story and a story written by Bret Harte, "The Luck of Roaring Camp." Roaring Camp was a rough mining settlement in the early West. Drinking, gambling, and profanity were rampant. One Christmas Eve there was extra bustle far down at the end of the one street. An unwelcome babe was born to the camp cook. Impressed and touched, the miners brought crude gifts to lay at the child's cradle. They named him Luck. As the child grew he so captured the hearts of those rough miners that Roaring Camp was transformed. Later this little child died when a dam broke and swept the camp away. The memory of Luck of Roaring Camp continued to control the lives of those men.

In his later years the Babe of Bethlehem also died. His humble birth taught the world the value of true riches. His death brought peace and hope to mankind.

Dear Savior, be born in my heart. Make it a temple fit for thee. Amen.

God's Work for Me

For our sake he made him to be sin who knew no sin, so that in him we might become the righteousness of God. 2 CORINTHIANS 5:21

Sin stood as a wall separating man from fellowship with God. Man was helpless and unable to restore this relationship. In his infinite love God determined to remove that barrier.

In his plan of love, conceived "before the foundation of the world," God promised that Jesus Christ should come to earth as a man. In human form he was to take man's place and do what we could not do—fulfill God's will and work perfectly. By his perfect life, sacrificial death, and triumphant resurrection he was to remove, once for all, that wall of separation between God and man.

The sinless Savior became one of us and took upon him our sin. When he knelt in Gethsemane, he prayed, "Not my will, but thine be done." When all his work on our behalf was complete and Jesus was about to give his life on the cross, he cried out, "It is finished." Jesus had paid the price of our sins to accomplish his Father's will and work for us. The Lamb of God had been sacrificed.

In Chicago the court ordered a landlord to lower the rent in his apartment house. He retaliated by cutting off the utilities. A lawsuit resulted. Later the landlord repented of his action, but had no money to pay the fine. The judge, anxious to solve the problem, offered personally to pay the fine, but a federal agency said that was illegal. Our debt, however, was paid by our Savior when he fulfilled God's will. We can stand before God as if we had never sinned.

Blessed Savior, thank you for coming, and for taking my guilt and sin. Amen.

A Man Who Is God

In the beginning was the Word, and the Word was with God, and the Word was God.

JOHN 1:1

One of the main differences between other religions of the world and Christianity is that the followers of these other religions must reach out to their gods, while in Christianity our God reaches out to us. He reveals himself to us in the person of Jesus Christ. He is Emmanuel, "God with us." He came to us!

Jesus did the works of God. Of his own ministry he said, "The blind see, the lame walk, lepers are cleansed, the deaf hear, the dead are raised, and the poor hear the good news." He forgave sins.

Scripture assigns to Jesus the attributes of God. *Eternal:* "before all things." *All-powerful:* "All authority is given to me." *Every-*

where-present: "Lo I am with you always."
All-knowing: "He knew what was in man."
Unchangeable: "Jesus Christ, the same yesterday, and today and forever."

Jesus was given the names of God, and was worshipped. "My Lord and my God." "At the name of Jesus every knee shall bow." "God manifest in the flesh."

Jesus himself claimed to be God. He accepted divine names and worship without protest. He had mastery over nature, controlling winds and waves. Paul wrote, "He was designated Son of God by his resurrection."

With Peter we can say, "Thou art the Christ, the Son of the living God," and with Thomas, "My Lord and my God."

My Savior, though I do not deserve it, come and be with me always. Amen.

The God Who Was Man

The Word became flesh and dwelt among us.
JOHN 1:14

Jesus Christ is God and also true man. He was born of the virgin Mary. He experienced all the human bodily needs we do. He needed to eat, drink, sleep, exercise, and care for his body as we do. Sometimes he was sad. We believe that Jesus was a strong man, yet on at least two occasions we know he wept. He was tempted. He suffered and died. The Apostle Paul wrote of him, "There is one God, and one mediator between God and man, himself man, Christ Jesus."

Jesus was a good man. He was a man in every respect except without sin. His life was perfect. As a lad at Nazareth, "He was obedient to his parents." All through life he left us a perfect example.

However, the main reason that Jesus became man was so that he could fulfill the law for us and suffer and die in our stead. St. Paul explains this, "Being found in human form he humbled himself and became obedient unto death, even death on a cross."

There is a parallel between the life of our Savior, and that of Kagawa, the beloved Japanese Christian. In order to minister more effectively to the poor in his land, he left the comforts of his home to live among them. Because of privations Kagawa became ill and died. Our Savior did not minister to our needs from a distance, but left his heavenly home to live among us and bore our sins to his death.

Savior, thanks for thy perfect life, and for thy sacrificial death. Amen.

A Double Ownership

You call me Teacher and Lord; and you are right, for so I am.   JOHN 13:13

Jesus paid a tremendous price for our redemption. With his precious blood, his innocent sufferings and death, he has bought and freed us. We belong to him by virtue of a double ownership—creation and salvation. Therefore, Jesus is our Lord and Master. He should command central place in our lives. Everything should revolve about him in our plans and choices.

A rich young man had inherited a large estate on the shores of Lake Michigan. There he decided to build a large mansion which would be his dream house. He made plans which included everything he ever wanted. When he took his plans to an architect, he was advised that some drastic changes would have to be made.

Being a willful young man he was offended at this. He told the architect to build according to his plans. So the house was built. When the young man came to inspect it, he was thrilled to find his plans carried out precisely. Every detail was perfect. Then the blow fell. When he wanted to inspect the second floor, he discovered to his great dismay, that he had forgotten to include a stairway! His lovely home had to be torn up and rearranged because of his oversight.

Just so, our lives can come to drastic disappointment if we make plans and decisions according to our selfish purposes, and leave Jesus Christ out. He is our Lord and Master. Lives of happiness must include him.

Dear Savior, I want to belong to thee. Direct my life. Amen.

Pattern of Perfection

He went about doing good. ACTS 10:38

Jesus' life is the Christian's pattern for holy living. Peter referred to him as a "Lamb without blemish or spot." He leads the way for us. Not that by following a good example we merit God's approval and be saved, but that our lives may see true holiness and strive toward that goal.

For children there is no better ideal than Jesus. He was obedient to his parents. He showed, even as a twelve-year-old, a deep dedication to his Father's house and kingdom. His ministry lasted only three years, but it can be laid along our lifetime as the ideal Christian life. It began with baptism. He was baptized, not because he needed to be, but to go with us throughout our human experience, and to sanctify our baptism.

Jesus was a gentle, patient person. He showed anger only in the cause of righteousness. He was falsely accused, but made no reply. His response to those who tormented him was simply to pray for them. "When he was reviled, he did not revile in return." His love endured and conquered. His only concern was the accomplishment of his messianic mission. Jesus was unyielding in his pursuit of his Father's will. When Satan came to divert him, Jesus prevailed with power. His defeat of Satan is our best pattern for victory over temptation.

Thus throughout life Jesus gave us a beautiful example. We can justly make our own the words of the hymn, "I long to be like Jesus, meek, loving, lowly, mild."

Dear Savior, help me to live a holy life like thine. Amen.

Such Love Is Costly

Having loved his own who were in the world, he loved them to the end.   JOHN 13:1

Jesus was acquainted with grief and suffering. The sinless One lived in a sinful world. He was fully aware of all the sin around him in the world he came to save. It caused him grief. The faithful pursuit of his mission was constantly threatened by opposition. Truly he was "a man of sorrows and acquainted with grief."

Our Savior suffered most of all the last days of his life, and particularly on the day of his death. He experienced the scorn and ridicule of the people. He felt the pain of the fist, the whip, the thorns, the nails, the cross, the sword. To him death must have come as sweet relief. Most of us shower our love upon, and are willing to sacrifice for those who cause us joy and gratification. But Jesus loved the loveless. He died for his enemies. Man's sin, and the Savior's love, combined to force our Lord to his death.

This was not a coward's death. He died courageously and triumphantly. He said of his life, "No one takes it from me, but I lay it down of my own accord."

During World War II a submarine captain was wounded on deck by a surprise air attack. Because he lay helpless and knew there was no time to carry him below if his ship and his men were to escape, he ordered the hatches closed and the sub lowered. This meant his death, yet concern for his men prevailed. To fulfill his love Jesus went to his death; and because he died, we are forgiven and reunited with God.

Precious Savior, I stand in awe at thy love. Thanks for thy sacrificial death. Amen.

His Grave and Mine

Where now, O grave, is the victory you hoped to win?   I CORINTHIANS 15:55 PHILLIPS

The fearful ordeal was over. The Savior's body was silent in death. Now some of his friends came forward. Two influential men in the community asked permission to bury the body of Jesus. Joseph, a wealthy man of Arimathea, a good man and a member of the Council, assisted by Nicodemus, also a Council member, who came to see Jesus one night, buried the body in Joseph's new tomb. So there was a Joseph at either end of Jesus' life, one to shelter him at birth, and the other provided for him after his death.

Graves and cemeteries have never been cheerful places. They represent sadness, the sadness of parting. Death means separation—separation of body and soul, but also separation of dear ones. It is always difficult to follow those we love to that sacred spot and return without them.

That is only one side of the picture, however. We know our Savior did not stay in the grave. He was raised triumphantly from death and the grave some 36 hours later. Though they had made the grave "secure," they neglected to reckon with the Lord of Life. He came forth alive.

Think what this meant to Joseph. Jesus had occupied his grave. How almost eagerly he could look forward to sleeping where Jesus had lain. Jesus had buried his sins and hallowed his grave. He emerged alive forevermore. The same blessing is in store for us.

Kind Savior, be near me in my dying hour. Thanks for the comfort of thy resurrection. Amen.

To the Enemy's Capitol

He descended into the lower parts of the earth.

EPHESIANS 4:9

When Adolf Hitler conquered France in World War II he drove his forces all the way to Paris, the capitol city of France. There he made great show of his power as he paraded down the Champs D' Elysee and through the Arche De Triomphe. Every Frenchman in the world that day knew that Hitler had indeed conquered France. In far greater power and glory, and in the cause of righteousness, Jesus Christ, conqueror of Satan and his kingdom of sin and death, descended to hell, the capitol of the kingdom of darkness.

Jesus did not descend to hell to give those consigned there a second chance. He went there to display his victory at Calvary. Satan and all his demons were to know that they had met their conqueror in Jesus Christ. As prophesied in the garden of Eden, the Son of God had "bruised Satan's head" when he laid down his life on the cross. The result is that Satan and all his agents know Jesus Christ. "Jesus I know," said the demon at Ephesus. "Even the demons believe and shudder," wrote James. They know and fear the name of Jesus.

There is great comfort in knowing that the power of Satan has been destroyed for those who share by faith Christ's victory on the cross. The important thing for us, therefore, if we are to overcome the Evil One, is to know Christ's victory and share it. The gospel declares this glorious message. What a wonderful Savior we have!

Fortify me, Lord, and reassure me daily that thy victory over Satan is also mine. Amen.

God Said Amen

He was designated Son of God in power ... by his resurrection from the dead. ROMANS 1:4

When the Old Testament high priest, on the great Day of Atonement went behind the veil into the Holy of Holies with the sacrifice, the congregation waited expectantly for his return. Should any point in the law of the sacrifice in that holy place be violated, the people knew they would never see their high priest alive again. When, however, they saw him emerge through the veil, they knew that their sacrifice had been accepted, and their sins had been forgiven by God. God's benediction of peace settled upon them.

Our great high priest, Jesus Christ, went into the tomb, behind the veil of death, with his perfect sacrifice for our sins. When he emerged alive, it became manifest that God had said, "Amen" to all that Jesus had said, did, and claimed to be. God had accepted Christ's sacrifice, and our sins were forgiven.

The resurrection of Jesus Christ is our proof that truly "God through Christ has reconciled us to himself." Through his resurrection Jesus was established as the Son of God. This is the power base from which we can receive strength to defeat our natural inclination to sin, and to live dedicated Christian lives. This is the assurance that we too shall be raised.

A Christian missionary in India and a Moslem were discussing their religions. "We know where our leader is buried, but you do not," said the Moslem.

Replied the missionary, "That's just the point, we have a living Lord."

Mighty God, fill me always with the power of my Savior's resurrection. Amen.

Homeward Bound

I am ascending to my Father and your Father.
JOHN 20:17

The day of parting had come. It was an experience Jesus' disciples had dreaded. The Savior had announced his leaving, and it made the hearts of his followers heavy. So, trying to comfort them, he explained, "It is to your advantage that I go away, for if I do not go away, the Counselor will not come to you." The day came, and the Savior led his disciples to the Mount of Olives near Bethany. There he lifted his hands in blessing upon them and was taken up into heaven.

The disciples were like men transfixed. They just stood looking heavenward. It took the appearance of angels to bring them back to reality. Although the Christian life cannot be spent piously gazing heavenward, it is true that Jesus' ascension teaches us that we must let the promise of heaven inspire our lives, our thoughts and deeds. "Seek the things that are above, where Christ is."

When an artist begins a landscape scene, he always paints the sky first. He does this because the sky gives light, color, and inspiration for the whole landscape. Likewise in life, the prospect of heaven gives light, meaning, and inspiration to all we experience. Heaven gives perspective and purpose. It becomes our goal.

Jesus, our priceless treasure, has preceded us into heaven. He invites us to follow, and has shown us the way. With eyes of faith on this goal, our constant theme can be, "Heaven is my home."

Blessed Savior, inspire my life with hope of heaven and the certainty of being with thee. Amen.

Our Spokesman in Heaven

If any man sin, we have an Advocate with the Father, Jesus Christ the Righteous.   I JOHN 2:1

Before our Savior ascended to heaven, he told his disciples, "Lo, I am with you always." A Chinese lad by the name of Lo heard the pastor read that verse. His immediate, happy response was, "Jesus promised to be with me always." Each of us can put our name into that promise, and it will be equally as true as it was for Lo. Although we know Jesus is with us here, Scripture says he is at the right hand of the Father in heaven. "Jesus . . . sat down at the right hand of God."

A story tells of a princess who loved to travel among the people of her father's realm. She saw their poverty and need, and she thought of her father's abundance. "Why don't you make your needs known to your king?" the princess asked the people.

"We do not know how to ask the king," was their reply.

"Just tell me what you need and I will ask the king," was her promise.

The people knew they would have a good representative because the princess had been among them, and she had the ear of her father, the king.

At the Father's right hand Jesus has the place of power and authority. There our Savior, who took our place at Calvary, represents us and prays on our behalf. He is our Advocate. What joy and assurance! Jesus, our Savior, is interceding for us before his Father's throne in heaven.

Savior, I thank thee for praying for me. I have no righteousness but thine. Amen.

What Time Is It?

Then they will see the Son of man coming in a cloud with power and great glory.   LUKE 21:27

Some day, we know not when, Jesus will return and we will see him face to face! Accompanied by the holy angels he will gather all people who have ever lived, "from one end of heaven to the other." Our Lord shall sit on his glorious throne judging with equity and righteousness.

Then the great eternal separation will begin. Jesus will put the believers on his right, the unbelievers on his left. He will invite those on the right to go with him into the beautiful home he has prepared. Those on the left will experience everlasting separation from God. Joy on one side, and regret and sorrow on the other. No one goes to heaven because he is good, but because he believes in Jesus. No one goes to hell because he is so bad, but because he has turned his back on the Savior. Happy are those who love and trust in him.

The Bible clearly forecasts every detail of the final judgment except one — the day it will happen. "Watch, therefore, for you know neither the day nor the hour."

On one of his South Pole expeditions, Admiral Byrd and his party had to break camp very suddenly because of adverse weather conditions. They had time to pick up only a few articles of importance. At the moment of crisis their values were put into proper perspective. It was surprising what they could leave behind.

So we need to watch our time schedule and sense of values.

Blessed Savior, make me watchful and ready to meet thee, my Lord and my King. Amen.

Our Master Teacher

All that I have heard from my Father I have made known to you.   JOHN 15:15

A good landscape scene should include a way out of the picture: a road, a stream, a ray of light—something that will lead our vision out of the setting. Learning gives that quality to our lives. The word educate means to lead out —from confusion to clarity, from lack of understanding to knowledge.

Jesus was a great teacher. He knew the needs of his pupils and led them from the darkness of ignorance to the brightness of truth. As prophet and teacher his chief concern was to reveal the Father. God was not generally known as our Father until Jesus, our Brother, came to reveal him in that tender role. "No one knows the Father except the Son and anyone to whom the Son chooses to reveal him."

Jesus interpreted the Old Testament. He taught the commandments in New Testament light. The serpent in the wilderness was related to the cross. He established the Jonah story, binding it to his resurrection. He showed himself as the fulfillment of prophecy.

Jesus illustrated his lessons with examples from nature—sky, soil, flowers, animals. He pictured the Christian life in simple stories of servants, masters, tax collectors, priests. His lessons dealt with all facets of daily living—worship, love, property, bias. He pointed to himself as the only way out, the only hope of salvation. He proclaimed, "Come to me," "No one comes to the Father, but by me." Our Master Teacher led us to the truth.

Wonderful Teacher, show me day by day how to live my Christian life. Amen.

Where We Cannot Go

Jesus . . . at the right hand of God . . . intercedes for us. ROMANS 8:34

In his baptism Jesus was anointed by the Holy Spirit to be Prophet, High Priest, and King. As our High Priest he goes where we cannot go. This our Savior does in two ways.

First, the Old Testament priest offered sacrifices for the sins of the people, and for his own sins. Jesus offered himself for our sins, but not for his own, because he was sinless. As he died, he prayed, "Father forgive them." He needed no prayer for himself. His sacrifice was made on the altar of the cross. When he died he said, "It is finished." His work for our redemption was complete. Jesus made his priestly sacrifice for us "once for all," for all people, for all time. This we could not do. He went, as our High Priest, where we could not go.

Second, the Old Testament priest also prayed for the people. Jesus, our High Priest, prays for us. In the 17th chapter of John, known as the High Priestly prayer, he prayed for his disciples and us. The night following his feeding of the 5000 Jesus went up into the hills to pray, while the disciples were down on the stormy sea of Galilee. This is a picture of our situation today. Jesus, our High Priest, is praying for us in heaven, while we are confronted by the storms of life. He continues to go on our behalf where we cannot go.

Thanks, dear Jesus, for thy sacrifice for me. Mercifully keep me in thy prayers. Amen.

Under His Rule

Of his kingdom there will be no end.   LUKE 1:33

On the altar of one of the churches of Norway are three paintings. Each is the picture of a human heart, with an opening across the front.

The first picture shows the Savior holding a light which reveals much dust and tangled cobwebs. Inscribed under this picture is, "Jesus gives light."

The second picture represents Jesus with a red cloth in hand wiping away the grime. Written beneath this picture is, "Jesus cleanses."

The third heart-picture reveals the Savior seated upon a throne. Angels surround him. All is happiness and beauty. Under this picture it says, "Jesus reigns." This is a picture story of what happens when Jesus comes into the heart, sets up his throne, and reigns. Under his rule Jesus cleans away all sin, and controls our lives.

Jesus is a king indeed! Zechariah prophecied of his ministry, "Lo, your king comes to you." Words of true testimony were put into Pilate's mouth, "Here is your king." Paul referred to Jesus as the "King of kings."

As our king, Jesus wants to control us to our fingertips. He wants to rule our thoughts and desires. He wants to control our words and deeds. He wants to direct our feet and hands. He wants to inspire our emotions. Our king will also defend us from all evil. Under his reign he will lead us to happiness and peace.

Come into my heart, Lord Jesus. Rule and direct me in all things. Amen.

A Total Commitment

You are not your own; you were bought with a price.   I CORINTHIANS 6:19-20

When the Apostle Paul was writing to Titus, he told him that because the grace of God had appeared in the coming of Jesus Christ we should live "sober, upright, and godly lives." Jesus has completed his great redemptive work, "in order that I might be his own, live under him . . . and serve him." We are not our own. We have been purchased at great price. We owe him our lives.

David Livingstone was living in comfort and high esteem in England. Before him was a lifetime of self-satisfying success and distinction. However, gratitude for his Savior's love overwhelmed him, and when he heard of the need for the gospel in the dark continent, he left the comforts of home and spent his life as a missionary in Africa, a trackless, untamed wilderness in those days. Although he experienced hard years of privation and ill-health, he faithfully carried the gospel to villages far and near. On a furlough trip back to England he was strongly urged to give up his strenuous efforts. He refused, and returned to the work he loved. There he labored until his death. David Livingstone felt he could never pay the debt of gratitude he owed his Lord.

The price of our redemption is the precious blood and the innocent sufferings and death of our blessed Savior. We can never repay him!

Give me many years, dear Lord, and strength with which to serve thee. Amen.

God's Work in Me

No one can say "Jesus is Lord" except by the Holy Spirit.
I CORINTHIANS 12:3

Jesus, our Savior, has done God's work for us. The Holy Spirit is doing God's work in us. We can rightfully wonder why there are so many millions in the world who do not know Christ, when he has done so much for their salvation. There is only one answer. The Holy Spirit has not had opportunity to do his work in their hearts. This is a sad situation, since the only way the Holy Spirit can operate is through the means of grace—the Word and the sacraments. Had we done a better job of spreading the message of the gospel, no doubt the situation would be different.

What is this work of the Holy Spirit? It begins with repentance—leading us to an awareness of our sins, a longing to be forgiven, and an honest desire to forsake sin. The Holy Spirit then leads the penitent to the cross of Jesus Christ, where forgiveness and salvation are assured. From that point the Spirit leads along the pathway of uprightness, gratitude, peace, and joy in the Christian life. Each step of the way is the work of the Holy Spirit in the Christian heart.

The Holy Spirit has only one function, and that is to lead us to Jesus Christ and to a life in his name. "No one can say 'Jesus is Lord' except by the Holy Spirit." This is the ultimate of God's work in us.

Spirit of God, work thy work in my heart. Lead me day by day to increased joy and peace in my Christian life. Amen.

About Face

God's kindness is meant to lead you to repentance. — ROMANS 2:4

Aesop's fables often teach us many important lessons. Such a one is the story of the cloud, the sea, and the sun. One bright, sunny morning a fluffy, white cloud was floating far up against the deep blue sky. Down below, the sea lay looking up at the the cloud. It whispered to itself, "I'm told that that cloud was once down here where I am. I wish I could get up there and float around so carefree." So the sea gathered all its might and tossed great ships like thimbles. It asked its cousin the wind for help, and together they piled up mountainous waves, until the sea finally dashed itself against the rocks and fell back defeated. It could not climb up into the sky. Suddenly the sea thought, "I'll ask the sun to help me." The sun agreed. So the sun sent down warm, noiseless rays upon the waters, and soon great portions of the sea were floating as clouds in the sky. This was accomplished by the great drawing and purifying power of the sun.

Like the sea, we are apt to labor under delusions of our own grandeur and power. We try to climb by our own merit to heights of righteousness and God's approval, only to learn how futile the struggle is. It is a hard decision to reach, since it involves an about-face of repentance. Yet we can know that this is God's way of leading us by his kindness, and the drawing power of his Son, to sincere and honest repentance. Defeated in our own attempts, we discover how helpless we are. Then we can experience the lifting power of God's love.

Lead me, kind Father, to discover how much I need to repent daily. Amen.

Believing Is Seeing

Faith is the assurance of things hoped for, the conviction of things not seen. HEBREWS 11:1

There isn't a court in the land that would convict on the basis of things not seen. Yet, more daring risks have been taken, more far-reaching decisions made on the basis of faith than on logic or reason. Who would dare commit his soul for eternity on any other basis than faith in God's promises?

One day a woman in dire physical distress came to Jesus. The crowd was pressing in on him. She thought, "If I can touch the hem of his garment I will be made well." She reached through the crowd to Jesus. Her outstretched finger displayed her faith, and her faith was rewarded. Jesus said, "Your faith has made you well."

The prodigal son knew his father would welcome him home. He took that journey of faith and was not disappointed.

Hebrews 11 lists a long line of heroes of faith. An unseen hand led Abraham into a strange land. Noah built a huge ship on dry land in a country where floods were unknown. Moses left the comforts of wealth and power to endure great hardships as he led God's people to the promised land.

When a penitent soul trusts completely in the righteousness promised by God through Jesus Christ, this is faith. Paul wrote Romans to prove that we are saved by "the righteousness of God apart from the law . . . through faith in Jesus Christ." God, the Holy Spirit, leads us to Jesus, and gives us saving faith in him.

Spirit of God, grant me faith. Help me to trust Jesus only for my salvation. Amen.

Undeserved Merit

They are justified by his grace as a gift, through the redemption which is in Christ Jesus. ROMANS 3:24

A severe quarrel had arisen between an ancient king and his queen. The queen was at fault, and a beautiful relationship of love was broken. Filled with wrath, the king gave orders that the queen should not be permitted in his presence. The queen was deeply distressed and sought some way she might regain her king's love. She might send a messenger with kind words. She might prepare a feast of the king's favorite foods. Or, she might put on her loveliest gown and parade before him. The queen knew it would all be futile.

At last she hit upon a happy plan. Taking their little child, the king's only son, in her arms she went boldly before the king. Seeing the love that poured upon his son from the eyes and heart of the mother, the king forgot his anger. The differences were dissolved, and peace was restored.

Sin broke our relationship with God. No overture we can make can restore that relationship. Only when we cling to God's Son, Jesus Christ, as our Savior, will that relationship and peace be restored. Then God declares us fully forgiven for Jesus' sake, crediting us with his righteousness. God's attitude toward us changes, and he looks on us in Christ as if we had never sinned. "In Christ Jesus you are all sons of God, through faith." This miracle of forgiveness and salvation is purely a gift of God's grace.

Lord Jesus, I need thy righteousness, for I have none of my own. Amen.

A New Beginning

A new heart I will give you, and a new spirit I will put within you.   EZEKIEL 36:26

Nicodemus was an influential man among his people. A member of the Jewish council, a teacher and a leader of the synagogue, he was a good man. As a strict Pharisee he was anxious to do what was right. Nicodemus respected Jesus and wanted to learn more about him and his teachings. Wishing to escape notice, however, he chose to visit Jesus after dark. In their conversation Jesus mentioned something Nicodemus could not understand or do anything about. Jesus told him, "You must be born again."

Ever since then, people have had difficulty with this "must" which Jesus emphasized that night. To be "born again" was so important,

Jesus said, that without it one could not even "see the kingdom of God." When God declares us righteous by faith in Christ, he changes his attitude toward us. In the new birth, however, God changes us! God, the Holy Spirit, gives us a new heart. He puts a new spirit within us. The Holy Spirit awakens within us a new understanding of God's will, gives us a new desire to do God's will, and sets our conscience at peace with God and man. In Christ we become new creatures. "If any one is in Christ, he is a new creation."

Jesus said Nicodemus, who was a good man, needed a new heart. We all do. That is why Jesus said, "That which is born of the flesh is flesh." Sinful by nature, we need to be born again to be a part of God's kingdom.

Lord, help me to remain in Christ, and let Christ be seen in me. Amen.

Christian Maturity

Every branch that does bear fruit he prunes, that it may bear more fruit.   JOHN 15:2

Jorgen Moe, the Norwegian bishop and author, wrote a poem entitled, "The Young Birch Tree." It pictured a pretty little birch tree growing close to one of the fjords of Norway. Each day the little tree tried to grow and spread its branches. But, standing where it was, it saw itself mirrored in the water upside down. So the tree thought it was growing downward day by day. Instead, through the years, it had become a tall, beautiful tree. The birds nested in its branches, and it stood as a picture of praise to God.

The Christian life can be like that birch tree. As God's grace ministers to us, we seem to grow downward in our own eyes, yet upward in the eyes of God and men. To be fruitful in God's kingdom, to live a life of praise to God, we need to feel his pruning knife often. The daily renewal, in which we daily experience sorrow for sin, and the joy of forgiveness, is necessary if we are to grow in grace. Through the constant strengthening of his Word and the Lord's Supper, God the Holy Spirit helps us to see ourselves in proper perspective, and to become fruitful and useful in his kingdom.

St. Paul has said it best. "That we no longer be children . . . rather grow up in every way into Christ." The sinful nature must give way to the new nature. Then we can express our Christian maturity by reflecting the love of God to those around us.

God, bless me with sincere humility and with love to thee and others. Amen.

Like a Mighty Army

"You are the Christ, the Son of the living God." ... "On this rock I will build my church."

MATTHEW 16:16, 18

The holy Christian church was founded by Jesus Christ on the confession that he is God.

The church is called holy because there through the Word of God and the sacraments the Holy Spirit produces faith and holiness in God's people.

The church is called universal or catholic because it is world-wide and one. Though there are many divisions, the Christian church is one, including believers in all groups, nations, and periods of time.

The church is called the Body of Christ because he is the Head. He gives the church his Spirit and power.

What shall be our relation to God's church? It is easy to lose sight of the real objective of the church and why we are in it. It may become for us just another club, or a place to work.

Three men, at the same job building a cathedral in New York City, were asked, "What are you doing?"

One answered, "I'm earning $20 a day."

Another said, "I'm mixing cement."

The third said proudly, "I'm helping build the cathedral of St. John the Divine."

We are part of a mighty army, engaged in an urgent, world-wide campaign for the Prince of Peace.

Holy Spirit, work thy miracles of grace in the church, beginning with me. Amen.

The Foundation of Our Faith

"Behold, the Lamb of God, who takes away the sin of the world!" JOHN 1:29

"Lamb of God" is the Bible's most descriptive name of our Savior. It pictures Jesus as God's sacrifice for the sins of all mankind. Martin Luther explained this very clearly when he said, "This is the foundation of our faith, that we know where our sins are laid. The law loads them on our conscience, but God lifts them away from us and places them upon the shoulder of the Lamb. Sin has only two places where it may rest, either upon thyself, or upon Christ. Choose, therefore, what it shall be."

With his blood our Savior paid the price of our sins. "The blood of Jesus, his Son, cleanses us from all sin." God himself buried Moses, the law-giver, and only he knows where. Similarly

God buried the sins of the penitent lawbreaker, and only he knows where! The Old Testament prophet Micah wrote, "Thou wilt cast all our sins into the depths of the sea."

For the penitent believer the promise is clear and complete, "If we confess our sins, he is faithful and just, and will forgive our sins." The first missionaries to the Eskimos in Labrador found no word to express forgiveness. They made a word which means "not-being-able-to-think-about-it-any-more." Jeremiah promised, "I will remember their sins no more."

Jesus' forgiveness is total. From "scarlet" to "white as snow," from "crimson" to "wool." Not a stain remains.

Lord Jesus, thanks for thy forgiveness. Help me to be forgiving too. Amen.

A Glorious Body

The Lord Jesus Christ will change our lowly body to be like his glorious body. PHILIPPIANS 3:21

Long ago Job, in the Old Testament, made some comments about life after death. His words are true and meaningful for every Christian today. Job said, "I know that my Redeemer lives." Then he went on to declare that he also knew that even though his body would return to the ground and be destroyed, some day he would stand upon the earth and see God. This remarkable statement is almost identical with one our Savior made before his death, "Because I live, you will live also." St. Paul expressed the same thought in his great resurrection chapter, "If there is no resurrection of the dead, then Christ has not been raised." The resurrection of Jesus assures us of our resurrection.

Therefore we need not fear the grave. One day we shall be raised. Our bodies, which have been subject to the ravages of sin, sickness, pain, violence, and death, will be made new, like Jesus' glorious resurrected body. Paul asks, "With what kind of a body do they [the risen] come?" He then answers his own question, "What is sown is perishable, what is raised is imperishable. It is sown in dishonor, it is raised in glory."

When the final day comes, our Lord will awaken our bodies, reunite them with our souls, and call us to be with him forever in his glorious mansions in heaven.

Savior, grant me a peaceful departure and a glorious resurrection. Amen.

Before God's Throne

Therefore are they before the throne of God, and serve him day and night within his temple.
REVELATION 7:15

How long is everlasting? It defies measurement, yet someone has tried to describe it in this way. Just imagine a mountain of fine sand taller than the highest mountain. Every thousand years a bird comes to pick up one tiny grain of that sand and flies off to deposit it in a particular place. When the bird has moved that entire mountain, this would be only the beginning of eternity.

Or, imagine a ball of steel the dimensions of the earth, and a fly crawling around the middle of it. When the fly has eroded this ball of steel into two halves, this would be only the beginning of eternity.

These descriptions are inadequate, yet they

give us some idea of the vastness of eternity, which never ends.

Those who have rejected faith in Christ will be separated from God through endless eternity.

In contrast, those who believe in Jesus until death will be permitted to see him face to face, and be in his presence through endless eternity. Words are inadequate to describe what it shall be to join the numberless white-robed host before the throne of God. We shall be with the angels and the saints of all ages, and experience freedom from sin, troubled conscience, and all earthly needs. All tears will be wiped away. Only continued joy in the presence of God! The prospect of heaven compensates for all earthly suffering.

Gracious God, keep me faithful all the way, and grant that I may be with thee in heaven forever. Amen.

Prayer Practices

Let the words of my mouth and the meditation of my heart be acceptable in thy sight, O Lord.

PSALM 19:14

The Savior wants us to bring our burdens to him. He commanded us to pray, taught us how to pray, and gave us a perfect model prayer. He has promised to hear and answer when we pray.

Prayer is heart-to-heart talk with God. Acceptable prayer involves the heart. The words spoken in such prayer become the expression of devout heart-meditation. We may come to God in prayer as children come to their father, and know he is waiting to hear.

We should always pray in Jesus' name. He is our mediator, who prays for us before the Father. Because he represents us there, we can pray with boldness and confidence, asking what is good for ourselves and others, even our enemies. Our prayer must be according to God's will and for his glory.

We are urged to pray at all times. As Christians we go through the day in an attitude of prayer. It is possible to think or sigh our prayers to God. Yet it is good to set special times during the day for prayer—morning, evening, before and after meals.

The Holy Spirit inspires us to pray. He makes us aware of our sins, reveals our needs, and reminds us of our blessings. He teaches us that it is often necessary to deny our prayers, and that God may delay the answer, or give us something better. If we live a truly humble, ardent prayer life, God will receive the glory.

God, make me strong in prayer, and may all the glory be thine. Amen.

Prayer Privileges

If you ask anything of the Father, he will give it to you in my name.   JOHN 16:23

Only they can call God their Father who are truly God's children. Jesus made us God's children, and brought us into such intimate fellowship with God that we can truly speak to him as our Father. Accordingly our relation to Jesus, our Brother, determines our relation to God, our Father. If we want to call God our Father, we must hold fast our faith in Jesus, his Son, our Brother. What a privilege it is for us to be permitted to pray this intimate, beautiful prayer! They are words that came from the lips of Jesus.

It is a privilege, likewise, to pray "our" Father. In that holy moment it is as if we join hands with believers all around the world. Together we look to our heavenly Father and pray with and for one another.

We pray this perfect prayer to a loving heavenly Father. We know our Savior is praying for us at his right hand. What a circumstance for boldness and confidence in prayer! Confident that the Father will hear us, we know that he will answer with what is for our best. A prayer privilege beyond compare!

The king's son broke a palace window with his ball. Those in charge started the slow process of notifying the king. When they finally were admitted into his presence the boy was already sitting on the king's knee telling him all about it. We have the privilege of going directly into our Father's presence.

Father in heaven, lead me to make all my needs known to thee. Amen.

A Holy God

Sanctify them in thy truth, thy word is truth.
JOHN 17:17

Our God is holy. Because he is holy he desires and deserves a holy people. Jesus taught this when he said, "You must be perfect as your heavenly Father is perfect." The first petition of the Lord's Prayer says that as God's children we are to live lives which reflect glory upon our heavenly Father. This does not mean that God's holiness depends on our behavior. It means that by our lives we are to show those around us the kind of God we have. None of us can estimate the importance of such witness. The world is in desperate need of knowing that there is a holy, righteous God who desires to deal with us in love. The world has seen so much of the profaning of God's name, and it is not impressed.

How can we give a positive witness of our God? God has given us a holy book. When the message of Holy Scriptures is preached and taught so that people everywhere turn to God in penitence and faith in the Lord Jesus Christ, then the world will know that our holy God is the God it needs. That the gospel is everywhere taught, and that our lives conform to it, is the responsibility of those who call God their heavenly **Father.**

In the early days of the church the Christians made such a clear testimony of their faith that unbelievers were impressed and exclaimed, "Behold how they love one another!" These early believers hallowed God's name.

Lord, bless the preaching of thy Word. Help me to live according to it. Amen.

A Chain Reaction

Pray the Lord of the harvest to send out laborers into his harvest. MATTHEW 9:38

In the tenth chapter of John Jesus compares himself to the shepherd, his followers to the sheep. He was not content with only a little flock, for he said, "I have other sheep that are not of this fold; I must bring them also."

When the Savior gave us the second petition he was thinking of those "other sheep." God's kingdom comes when the Word of God transforms our lives, and burdens our hearts for the souls of others. A contagion is thus created—a chain reaction. Using our godly lives, God brings others into the kingdom.

Alfred Tucker, a noted Scottish painter, felt he was not making the most of his life. One Sunday he heard his pastor's sermon on "The Other Sheep." That week he was painting the picture of a poor woman in rags, a little child clutched tightly in her arms. She was a picture of distress. As Tucker studied his picture, he suddenly thought, "Instead of painting pictures of lost, distressed people, why don't I go and help them?" Tucker became a missionary in Africa. There for many years he brought the light of the gospel to the people of that continent.

There are "other sheep" in far-off countries as well as right here at our elbows. Jesus' prayer that God's kingdom come to them is answered when Christ reaches into our hearts. The chain reaction can start with you.

God, create love in my heart, and give me a burden for the souls of others. Amen.

A Difficult Prayer

This is the will of God, even your sanctification.
I THESSALONIANS 4:3 KJV

Jesus did the will of his Father and it cost him his life. He fulfilled his Father's will perfectly. "Thy will be done on earth as it is in heaven." From a selfish point of view this is the most difficult of all prayers to pray. If we are to pray this prayer and really mean it as our Savior did in the Garden of Gethsemane the night before he died, it will require complete surrender of our sinful ambitions and desires.

The Savior always found joy in doing his Father's will. He said, "I seek not my own will but the will of him who sent me." Hebrews refers to this, "Jesus . . . for the joy that was set before him endured the cross."

The Apostle Paul happily resigned his will to God's. "It is no longer I who live, but Christ who lives in me." Paul had moved out and Christ had moved in. Although it is sometimes difficult for us to understand and accept God's will, we can be sure that it is always best.

This is the key to living the words Jesus taught, "Thy will be done on earth as it is in heaven." God's will is done when the influence of the Evil One is destroyed, and when we are kept steadfast in the Word of God. Translated into life this means that we daily become more and more like Jesus. When the Savior takes possession of our lives he increasingly overcomes our evil ways, and doing God's will increasingly becomes our greatest joy and desire.

Help me, Lord, to be submissive to thy will. Amen.

Cause for Gratitude

Have no anxiety about anything, but in everything by prayer and supplication with thanksgiving let your requests be made known to God.
PHILIPPIANS 4:6

It is difficult to understand the petition, "Give us this day our daily bread" unless we interpret it in light of the first part of the Lord's Prayer. This petition loses its meaning if we make it merely a prayer for food. In his explanation of these words Luther names 22 needs, and hints of others. This involves our total, physical, day-by-day existence. As a Christ-controlled life is the fulfillment of the first three petitions, a life totally dependent on God's providence, with Spirit-inspired gratitude, is the fulfillment of the fourth. This opens up a limitless depth of meaning for us.

One of the most difficult lessons to learn in the Christian life is that security and happiness do not depend on the amount of things we possess, but on our total dependence on God's providence, and on faith.

A young couple and their family moved into the community. Business was slow. They had to watch every penny. They were active in the church and had many friends. In spite of tight circumstances, they were happy and felt God took care of them. Later business improved. They moved in a world of affluence. They became too busy for the church, and God was forgotten. Happiness disappeared. They had more, but thanked God less. This story does not put a premium on poverty, but a value on our faith in God's providence.

In God's care, each day is a venture of faith, faith that God provides daily as we have need.

Lord God, increase my trust and gratitude. Provide for our daily needs. Amen.

A Dangerous Prayer

Be kind to one another, tenderhearted, forgiving one another, as God in Christ forgave you.

EPHESIANS 4:32

Can a prayer be dangerous? Jesus taught us to pray, "Forgive us our trespasses as we forgive those who trespass against us." We ask forgiveness from God in the same measure as we forgive others. If we refuse to forgive, then later pray this petition, we are in fact asking for our own condemnation. When we are unforgiving we are hardly in a position to ask forgiveness from God. Forgiveness from God requires penitence and a forgiving spirit. If we have no forgiveness, we have nothing.

When we refuse to forgive a neighbor, we not only build a wall between the two of us but also between ourselves and God. A wall of animosity had grown up between two brothers in a small-town congregation. The hatred had become so severe they refused to either meet or speak to each other. One Sunday, as they sat on opposite sides of the church, the pastor preached a stirring message on forgiveness and being forgiving. The Holy Spirit brought conviction to these brothers. Before the service ended one brother crossed over to ask forgiveness. There was reconciliation, and together they experienced the joy of God's forgiveness. The wall between them crumbled, and they were at peace with God and each other.

If we are forgiving, we will be forgiven, and we will discover that God's forgiveness is complete. Our Savior paid the full price. We can know and feel that peace has been established with God and our neighbor.

Savior, thanks for paying the price of my forgiveness. Help me forgive. Amen.

Times of Testing

Count it all joy, my brethren, when you meet various trials, for you know that the testing of your faith produces steadfastness. JAMES 1:2-3

Temptation can lead to sin, or it can strengthen faith.

In a well-guarded building at Homestake Gold Mine, chemists are at work purifying every ounce of gold produced. Modern methods have replaced the standard acid-test of former years, but with equally severe methods the precious metal is purified, and the result is pure gold.

God had assigned great responsibilities to Abraham. He was to be the patriarch of God's people. God knew what lay ahead for Abraham. His strong faith needed strengthening. To test his faith God asked Abraham to sacrifice his only son, a son through whom future generations were to come. Abraham followed God's directions and was strengthened for difficult experiences ahead.

King David was weak and needed strengthening. God sent trials, the death of one son, and rebellion of another. Later David wrote, "Before I was afflicted I went astray; but now I keep thy word."

The lustful wife of Potiphar set her eyes on Joseph, but Joseph refused her advances. God tempts no one to do evil, but will provide strength when such testing comes.

The greatest example of resisting temptation was set by our Savior. Deftly he used the sword of the Word to overcome Satan. That defense and victory is available for everyone.

God, grant me strength and victory when testing comes. Amen.

Final Security

The Lord will rescue me from every evil and save me for his heavenly kingdom. 2 TIMOTHY 4:18

The world God made was perfect. When he finished his creative work, Genesis says, "God saw everything he had made, and behold it was very good." Then people brought evil.

By our avarice and recklessness we have made fruitful soil into dry deserts, deep forests into wastelands and charred blackness. We have polluted our beautiful seas, lakes, and rivers, turned our fresh air into stinking smog. We are depleting our natural resources and threatening the survival of nature's species. Envy and theft attack our property and possessions. Permissiveness and lawlessness corrupt honor and discipline. Expediency displaces integrity.

Evil has brought its influence on the human body—sickness, pain, violence, death. It has preyed on the mind and conscience—sorrow, guilt, regret, insecurity, insanity. Evil has corrupted our social structure—poverty, racism, oppression, divorce, crime. Worst of all, evil has risen as a great wall between us and God. Sin and the promptings of Satan seem rampant.

We are captive like the people of Israel in the land of Babylon. We need deliverance. Dark as the picture is, God has promised to rescue us. There is temporary relief—conservation efforts, health care, law enforcement, social programs, and especially spiritual guidance and comfort. Total deliverance, however, will come when God calls us from this life. Then he will liberate us from all evil, and take us from this world of sorrow to himself in heaven.

Kind Father, sustain thy creation. Deliver me from sin, and save my soul. Amen.

Prayer Power

"Amen! Blessing and glory and wisdom and thanksgiving and honor and power and might be to our God forever and ever! Amen."

REVELATION 7:12

We are often discouraged in prayer. Like one who knocks on the door but does not wait for the answer, we often pray and do not expect results. We must remember that we have a prayer-answering God.

The kingdom is God's forever! One day as the king was riding in the country he came upon a poor lad. Invited into the carriage, the boy told of his family devastated by sadness and poverty. In desperation the boy was going to the king for help. "My boy, you are talking to the king," he was told. "The realm is mine. How can I help?" Earthly kings come and go, but our God rules forever.

The power is God's forever! Our world knows awesome power—atomic and hydrogen. Earthquakes and tornadoes erupt, but last only a few minutes. God's power is greater than all this together, and is forever.

The glory is God's forever! Jesus said that the Father answers our prayers for his glory. "Whatever you ask in my name, I will do it, that the Father may be glorified in the Son." God is glorified when his will is done.

Amen! This word means that God hears and accepts our prayers. It assures us of God's answer, in his way, in his time, and for our good. God's everlasting kingdom, power, and glory undergird our prayers. We can pray with confidence.

Father in heaven, hear my prayers. Bless me to thy glory, for Jesus' sake. Amen.

A One-Sentence Gospel

He who believes and is baptized will be saved.
MARK 16:16

Jesus gave us Baptism and the Lord's Supper. They manifest his love for us. In them he deals with us in a personal, one-to-one way, strengthening our weak, struggling faith. In Baptism he receives us into his kingdom and has established a covenant with us. When sin and doubt cloud our day, God invites us to take refuge in our baptismal covenant. When we receive the Lord's Supper, he reassures us personally that he loves us and forgives all our sins.

Baptism is defined as water used by God's command and with his Word. Jesus commanded that we be baptized into the name of the Holy Trinity. Through Baptism we are brought into the fellowship of the Father, and of the Son, and of the Holy Spirit. This is the gospel spoken in one sentence. We are baptized into everything we confess in the Apostles' Creed. The Word united with the water in Baptism is the same Word Paul describes as "the power of God for salvation." We are made God's children, members of his family.

Baptism does three things for us. It gives us the fullness of God's saving grace, forgiveness of sins, deliverance from the power of both death and the devil, and everlasting salvation. All this is assured in Jesus' promise, "He who believes and is baptized shall be saved." By Baptism we are brought into union with Christ. Paul says, "As many of you as were baptized into Christ have put on Christ."

Kind Savior, thanks for giving me faith and a new heart. Keep me steadfast in that faith. Amen.

Streams of God's Grace

We were buried ... with him by Baptism into death, so that as Christ was raised from the dead by the glory of the Father, we too might walk in newness of life. ROMANS 6:3-4

Baptism is not a one-time event, but a life-long covenant with God. It projects a daily, life-long union with Christ. In Baptism God promises forgiveness and a new life. He never fails. Our promise is twofold. We pledge a daily, life-long experience of sorrow and repentance for our sins, that our sinful nature may be put to death. We also pledge a daily, life-long experience of renewal of the life created in our Baptism. To survive and grow, our new spiritual life requires nurture and food each day, just as our physical bodies do. This new nature will mature when we live in God's Word, and experience and practice God's will. The Holy Spirit works in our hearts, through Word and Sacraments, to keep us faithful to our promise in Baptism.

All his life an old man had lived at the foot of a mountain. Each spring flowers had bloomed in his garden. Each summer the swallows had built nests under the eaves of his house. The flowers faded, and the birds flew south each fall. One thing did not change — the little spring which flows down the mountainside near his cottage. Its waters are as fresh and sparkling as when he was a boy. Day by day in this changing life God sends down on us the streams of his saving grace. Lamentations records, "His mercies . . . are new every morning." God asks only that we drink and grow in strength each day.

God, help me to remain in my baptismal covenant throughout my life. Amen.

A Memorial

Do this in remembrance of me.
I CORINTHIANS 11:24

The Lord's Supper is a memorial service, as Jesus specified. Each time we partake of Communion we vividly recall how Jesus suffered and died for us. We remember his agony in Gethsemane. We remember how they insulted, beat him, and crowned him with thorns. We remember the jeering crowd and the unjust sentence of death. We recall the heavy cross, the cruel nails which pierced his hands and feet, the bitter vinegar, the slashing sword, his wounded side. All this reminds us of his self-sacrificing love and his heroic death. In reality Holy Communion brings us face to face with the cross.

Our Savior's suffering and death remind us of the great weight of sin which caused it all. All the sins of all humanity of all time lay heavily upon his shoulders and brought agony and anguish to the Son of God. The cross stands as the emblem of his final victory and our total forgiveness.

During the Boxer uprising in China, there was great destruction of property. Sir John Bowring, the noted English hymn-writer, observed some of this as he cruised along the coast. He saw the outline of a demolished church, its tower and cross still looming high above the ruins. Deeply impressed at this sight, Bowring wrote his famous hymn, "In the cross of Christ I glory, towering o'er the wrecks of time." The cross stands as a strong reminder of Christ's victory over the ravages of sin. Holy Communion brings us to the foot of the cross.

Savior, thy cross was cruel, but it brings us peace, joy and gratitude. Amen.

A Testimony

As often as you eat this bread and drink this cup, you proclaim the Lord's death until he comes. — I CORINTHIANS 11:26

Our very act of partaking of the Lord's Supper becomes a testimony. A testimony of what we need and the answer to our need. It means that we are publicly taking our stand as sinners saved by grace. We are declaring our faith in Christ. When we receive the sacrament, the Apostle Paul says, we are proclaiming, or preaching, the Lord's death. Partaking of Holy Communion is a sermon on the death of our Savior, a message too precious to keep to ourselves.

In this sermon we are telling the world that by his death Jesus has atoned for our sins and has set us free from guilt. The sermon proclaims our joy and gratitude for God's mercy and forgiving love. We want the world to know the Savior has promised to come again some day, and the best way to prepare for his return is to remain with him in union and fellowship, which Communion offers.

A native African traded with some American tourists for a sundial. He did not know what it was, that to be of use it had to stand in the open sunlight. Wanting to keep it bright and shiny, he wrapped it up in a blanket and hid it in his hut. The Lord's Supper is one of our most precious possessions. We must not neglect it and hide it by lack of attendance, but take advantage of the opportunity it offers to proclaim aloud its blessings.

Jesus, I know thou wilt come again. By my regular participation in Holy Communion make me a faithful witness of thy death until then. Amen.

Proof of Forgiveness

"This is my blood . . . which is poured out for many for the forgiveness of sins." MATTHEW 26:28

In the Lord's Supper God gives us visible proof of his forgiving mercy. It is powerful evidence that our sins are forgiven. Sometimes the hardest thing in the world to believe is that our sins are forgiven. Satan tempts us to doubt God's promises. The burden of sin which we bring to the cross is so heavy that it seems impossible to lay down. But here at the Lord's table Jesus offers us his body and blood, "given and shed for you for the remission of sins." We have the assurance that Jesus blots out our iniquities. The sacrament becomes a great comfort to troubled souls. It strengthens our faith. The dominant mood of the communicant is joy and gratitude, for the peace which floods the soul.

A young couple settled as pioneers on the prairie. They became friendly with the nearby Indians. The man and the tribal chief sealed their friendship by stamping their fingerprints in their own blood upon a piece of paper. Often the husband would have to be away for supplies, leaving his wife and children alone. During those long nights she would hear the warlike cries of the Indians echoing through the hills, and it made her tremble with fear. Then she would open the chest and find the paper containing the covenant of blood. It was a promise of peace, and her heart was reassured and at rest. In a much greater way Jesus strengthens our faith through the Holy Sacrament.

Dear Savior, I come to Holy Communion convicted of sin. Cleanse me and give me joy. Amen.

Hungry and Thirsty

Let a man examine himself, and so eat of the bread and drink of the cup.   I CORINTHIANS 11:28

The Lord's Supper is the most hallowed gift God gives to us in this life—the body and blood of God's Son. We are receiving heavenly food. It is not an act which we may enter into lightly. St. Paul tells us to examine ourselves. This means that we should ask ourselves if we are truly penitent and desire to forsake sin. We should ask ourselves if we believe in Christ and desire to serve him more fully. We should ask ourselves if we believe the words of Jesus, "Given and shed for you for the remission of sins"—that in Holy Communion we receive Christ's body and blood, for the forgiveness of sins. If we can honestly answer yes to these questions, we may know that we are worthy guests at the Lord's table, however unworthy we may feel.

Some stay away from Communion who should go. They feel unworthy. Communion is much too sacred for them. If we wait until we feel totally worthy, perhaps we will never go. Communion is gospel, not law. The more unworthy we feel, longing for God's mercy and for power to win victory over sin, the more worthy we may be to receive God's grace. We may accept the body and blood of Christ as proof of God's love and know the joy of Holy Communion. Jesus said, "Blessed are those who hunger and thirst for righteousness, for they shall be satisfied."

God, make me a worthy guest when I receive Holy Communion. Amen.